The
PALM
READING
GUIDE

An Hachette UK Company
www.hachette.co.uk

First published in Great Britain in 2019 by Ilex,
an imprint of Octopus Publishing Group Ltd
Carmelite House
50 Victoria Embankment
London EC4Y 0DZ
www.octopusbooks.co.uk
www.octopusbooksusa.com

This edition published 2024

Text Copyright © Frank C. Clifford 2019
Design and Layout Copyright © Octopus
Publishing Group Limited 2019

Distributed in the US by
Hachette Book Group
1290 Avenue of the Americas
4th and 5th Floors
New York, NY 10104

Distributed in Canada by
Canadian Manda Group
664 Annette St.
Toronto, Ontario, Canada M6S 2C8

Publisher: Alison Starling
Commissioning Editor: Zara Anvari
Managing Editor: Rachel Silverlight
Junior Editor: Ellie Corbett
Contributing Editor: Kate Latham
Art Director: Ben Gardiner
Designer: Studio Polka
Assistant Production Manager: Lucy Carter

Frank C. Clifford asserts the moral right to be
identified as the author of this work.

ISBN 978-1-78157-945-9

Printed and bound in China

10 9 8 7 6 5 4 3 2 1

All reasonable care has been taken in the
preparation of this book, but the information
it contains is not intended to take the place of
any advice, counselling or treatment given by
a qualified practitioner. Any application of the
ideas and information contained in this book
is at the reader's sole discretion and risk.

MIX
Paper | Supporting
responsible forestry
FSC
www.fsc.org FSC® C008047

Frank C. Clifford is a London-based palmist and astrologer who has studied, taught
and written on both subjects for more than 30 years. His media work has included
documentaries with the BBC, Channel 5 and for Danny Boyle's feature film *Sunshine*,
being profiled in the *Daily Express* and the *Guardian* (who dubbed him 'palmist to the
stars'), and working with Universal Studios and Oxford University Press. One of his
astrology columns was even featured in an episode of *EastEnders*. His palmistry books
have been published in nine languages and *Palmistry 4 Today* was heralded
by many as the modern textbook on the subject. Frank lectures internationally and runs
Certificate and Diploma courses (online and in person) and weekend seminars via his
popular London School of Astrology, which now has divisions in China, Japan
and several Latin American countries. In 2012, Frank received a lifetime achievement award
for his work, which was followed by a writing honour in 2016. He has written for and
edited *The Mountain Astrologer* magazine.

www.frankclifford.co.uk   www.londonschoolofastrology.com

The PALM READING GUIDE

Frank C. Clifford

ilex

Contents

The Life Line

DRIVE, PASSION & AMBITION   22

The Head Line

LOGIC, CREATIVITY & MENTAL STRENGTH   36

The Heart Line

LOVE, SEX & RELATIONSHIPS 58

The Fate Line

WHERE ARE YOU GOING IN LIFE? 80

The Minor Hand Lines & Markings 100

The Language of the Hand

Your hands are living mirrors, reflecting your personality, needs and drives. They reveal your personal philosophies, and the talents you have inherited, as well as the ones that you are in the process of developing. Your hands show the important events and people from your past, and they give insights into the person you are today.

So, in many ways, your hands are your own unique personal autobiography, but not all the chapters have been written yet. Your hands chart the key moments, character traits and behaviours that have shaped your past, and reveal those that could influence your present and your possible future. The choices you make, and your responses to the events and people you encounter, all impact upon your life, and in turn they can alter the lines on your palms, too. The decisions, actions and reactions you make today will show in your hands tomorrow.

While palm reading can sometimes foretell upcoming events (after all, we can be quite predictable in many ways), the real secret to palmistry is that self-knowledge via your hands gives you control over your life. By gaining a greater awareness of your character and past actions through palmistry, you will learn how to influence your own future. Your hands reflect this two-way process and are a living testament to the power you have to shape your destiny.

THE LINES OF DESTINY

In this book you will learn how to read the 'language' of the lines and markings on your palms. You will learn how to use these markings – along with the shapes and proportions of your hands and fingers – to help you choose the most rewarding paths ahead.

You'll read about the major palm lines (the life line, heart line, head line and fate line) as well as the minor lines and special markings on your hand. You'll find out what the lines (their shape, dominance and course) reveal about you. All these features provide clues about the key areas of your life: your career prospects and talents, your love life and relationship needs, and your personality traits and motivations.

Learning to read palms opens up a whole world of insight. As you look at your palms in front of you, remember that the power of palmistry is not in predicting an unalterable future or fixed set of character traits. The magic of palmistry is that knowledge of your hands will help you make better decisions based on who you truly are and how you want your life to be.

HOW TO TAKE A HANDPRINT

Follow these steps to take a handprint. You'll need a tube of black water-soluble block printing ink, a sheet or pad of A4 or A3 paper (ideally 100 or 150gsm), a small printer's roller (or rolling pin), an art board or shiny magazine cover, and a hand/kitchen towel. It is best not to wash your hands before making prints.

1. Squeeze out a small amount of the ink onto the board or magazine and spread it thinly across the board/magazine with the roller (or rolling pin).

2. When the roller is evenly covered in ink, roll it over your palm (from your wrist to the fingertips). Ensure the centre of the palm is inked (sometimes a hollow centre can be tricky to print).

3. Place a towel under the paper. Relax your hand by shaking it gently and placing the palm down onto the paper. (You may

wish to draw around your palm with a pencil.) Press firmly to ensure the whole palm and fingers make an impression, then lift up carefully without smudging the print.

4. Repeat these steps with the second hand, then write the person's name, which hand they write with and the date of the print. Take a set of prints every year to see the developments.

WHICH HAND SHOULD I READ?

Most palmists look at both hands to provide a more complete picture of their client's temperament. Traditional palmists believe the two hands show different facets of one's personality. The markings shown on the left hand show your potential while markings on the right will reveal how much of this potential you tap into. Essentially, the left is what you are born with; the right tells you what you make of yourself. Many modern palmists don't believe it is as simple as this – they see potential everywhere in the hand and understand that lines change on both hands as time passes.

In my experience, the left hand – regardless of whether you are right- or left-handed – will always reveal more about your real self, who you are deep inside and behind closed doors. It is this hand that reveals your psychological dynamics and motivations – particularly those formed by early experiences. It shows the events that you internalize and the deeper issues and emotions that you ponder, analyse and reflect upon. Usually only those closest to you whom you trust – family, partners, best friends – will get to encounter the person you really are (your insecurities, private dreams, childhood issues). This is the person revealed in your left hand.

The right hand is who you are in public, when socializing and 'on show', consciously wishing to project an image. Markings on this hand will show the abilities that you manifest in your working life and how you can achieve success financially and professionally. For example, the right hand can show fame, success and riches – the sort that can be measured in public terms – but the left hand shows the extent of your personal sense of fulfilment and spiritual purpose.

Interpreting Your Hand

When you start palm reading, you'll begin to recognise the differences in the size, shape, texture and flexibility of people's hands, all of which reveal so much about them.

FIRST IMPRESSIONS

Size You can check the size of your hands by comparing them to the length of your face. An average hand should extend from the chin to the middle of the forehead.

If your hands are large, you have an ability to focus on detailed or intricate work. Your actions are slower than those around you, as you take your time to do things 'just right'. You can be a thoughtful, considerate and attentive partner.

If your hands are small, you think or act faster than those around you. In love, you won't have patience for someone who can't match your speed or live in the fast lane. At work, you see the overall picture and the finishing line, but may suffer from not attending to detail.

Skin texture Before assessing the skin texture, consider the person's age and the work they do. Coarse skin can be found on those of you who may not be the most sensitive or diplomatic with others. You are, however, able to cope with most things that life throws your way, and you have an ability to 'rough it' when necessary. When the skin is soft it shows an appreciation of the finer things, as well as an artistic bent. When very soft, you may be a little too fond of the good life and willing to let others do everything for you.

Flexibility How flexible are your hands and fingers? Firm hands show a purposeful temperament, while stiff hands reveal stubbornness.

Supple hands show adaptability, but flabby hands reveal a personality that can be easily dominated. Flexible fingers and fingertips are found on adaptable, 'easy come, easy go' people, while stiff fingers and fingertips show a rigid approach to life.

Hand shape Your hand's shape will reveal your basic motivations. Many modern palmists use the four elements – fire, earth, air and water – to classify the four major hand types, although some people's hands are a mix of two types.

The hand shape is an assessment of the shape of the palm and the length of the fingers. First, measure the palm from the wrist to the base of the middle finger and compare it to the width of the palm (from the outside of the palm to the fleshy mound lying beside the thumb). Square palms have measurements that are very similar and reveal a grounded and productive person. Rectangular palms (where the palm's length is greater than its width) show someone driven by passion or emotion.

Finger length is best determined by measuring the middle finger from the back of the hand (from knuckle to fingertip) and seeing how this measures up to the length of the palm (from the wrist to the base of the middle finger). Fingers are considered long when the middle finger is of equal or greater length to the palm. With long fingers, you are either intuitive and emotional (rectangular palms) or analytical and full of ideas (square palms). With short fingers, you are action-orientated either with spontaneous enthusiasm (rectangular palms) or a steady, solid practicality (square palms).

Fire, Earth, Air or Water Hand?

★ FIRE HAND

How to Tell: Long palm, shorter fingers, firm hand, deep lines
Key Attributes: Confident, passionate, impulsive

Love Your need for excitement is most apparent in relationships. You seek partners who are pioneers, prepared to push back the boundaries. For you, sex is a natural and necessary way of expressing your feelings. Your need for variety can lead to a seven-year itch as you bore easily and crave new challenges. You hate settling down into a fixed routine – predictability will sound the death knell of any relationship.

Personality You are driven to excitement and adventure. You seek a quest, but life is frustrating when there are no dragons to slay or causes to fight. Faith is an important theme in your life. It motivates you to live life to the fullest, to gamble on hunches and make big leaps that require courage and risk. Energy and enthusiasm are traits that you have in abundance.

Work For you, a job needs to be a calling. You need enlightening work that you feel passionate about. Often money is a means to an end, and you prefer glory and acclaim over financial security. You thrive in a job that puts you centre stage. You can inspire others but should avoid careers such as politics and the law in which diplomacy and patience are prerequisites.

★ EARTH HAND

How to Tell: Square palm, short fingers, very firm or fleshy hand, deep lines
Key Attributes: Practical, logical, honest

Love You are a loyal and dependable partner who offers security and comfort. Expressing your emotional needs may be tough, so you may sometimes feel lonely or misunderstood. You should learn to articulate your physical and emotional needs more. Partners will benefit from understanding that financial security is important to you, and that you need to establish foundations before you can venture forth, make a move or take risks.

Personality You succeed by applying yourself systematically, working hard and planning ahead. You are intent on constructing a firm foundation for your future. Taking risks is usually for others: you hate to waste time, money or energy. Creature comforts are important and you are motivated by financial reward, which gives you the security you crave. You strive for routine and a predictable, manageable world.

Work Never one to believe something without seeing it for yourself, you like to learn from hands-on application and first-hand experience. You work practically and methodically to absorb new concepts. Work that gets you back in touch with the physical realm, such as building, cooking and gardening, will be therapeutic and give you results that you can see. Try to avoid a build-up of stress, learn to unwind and express yourself through physical activity.

★ AIR HAND

How to Tell: Square palm, long fingers, long or clear lines
Key Attributes: Expressive, curious, logical

Love Partners soon discover that, although you have bags of charm and a quick wit, you sometimes need to disengage from them. Ideas, observations and discussions are more interesting to you than emotional dramas, so you need a partner who fires up your mind and is not afraid of a healthy argument to clear the air. You may be forced to probe your deeper emotions, which you usually keep safely locked away.

Personality You are a 'Peter Pan', full of youthful enthusiasm and curiosity. You seek to understand life and are motivated by finding answers. New ideas are constantly on the horizon, but trying to juggle them all could lead to little being accomplished. Set clear, realistic goals but keep a variety of avenues open. Putting pressure on yourself to be all things to all people will cause nervous tension and irritability.

Work For you, your work needs to be stimulating and teach you things you never knew. A career in the communication fields is perfect, and whether you write, teach, sell or work with computers, you will always have your phone and diary to hand. You will likely do a number of jobs (often at the same time) but your challenge is to produce concrete results and stay in one position long enough to really make your mark.

★ WATER HAND

How to Tell: Long palm, long fingers, soft hands, delicate or numerous fine lines
Key Attributes: Intuitive, sensitive, emotional

Love Protect yourself against negative, needy people who can pull you down and chip away at your self-confidence. Sometimes you find it easy to lose yourself in relationships, to take the form that your partner wishes rather than standing firm. But who's really controlling whom? You have a strong need to make emotional contact with a partner and this can make you manipulative as well as malleable. Sooner or later you will realise that you can share yourself without giving up your identity or trying to force others to change.

Personality You feel things more deeply than most and are able to tap into your emotions as well as the emotional state of others. You have a strong need to understand hidden motivations, raw emotions and life's mysteries. You are a sensitive, impressionable, nurturing and caring friend. Your biggest challenge is to fight your own self-doubt and pessimism. You must also learn to ask others for help directly rather than resorting to emotional blackmail.

Work This is satisfying only when you are receiving an emotional response from others. You need to serve, advise and support, so any caring profession would be ideal. All types of healing appeal to you, whether it is as a counsellor or building a bridge of understanding between opposing parties. Fashion and artistic work also attract your eye. Whatever your job, you bring sensitivity, empathy and understanding to your position.

Reading Your Fingers

Now that you know your hand type based on the general shape of your hand, look more closely at the length and appearance of your fingers. The fingers themselves can tell you huge amounts about a person – each finger representing different strengths and attributes.

FINGER	PLANET	ATTRIBUTE
Thumb	Mars	Energy, willpower
Index finger	Jupiter	Self-confidence, pride
Middle finger	Saturn	Responsibility
Ring finger	Sun, Venus	Creativity
Little finger	Mercury	Communication

The fingers show how you express your ideas and energies (as shown by the lines) and character (as seen by the hand shape). When one digit is significantly longer or shorter than expected, it suggests that the traits associated with that finger (listed above and opposite) fuel the personality and dominate the life.

Shake your hands and place them down on a flat surface. You'll notice that some fingers are close together while others sit apart. The spaces between individual fingers reveal current needs. When all of your fingers are held closely together, you are probably feeling conformist or conservative. When all of your fingers are spread out, you want to buck convention or shock. When the index finger sticks out towards the thumb, there's a desire to assert yourself personally (left hand) or professionally/socially (right hand). If your little finger juts out from the palm, there's a priority for personal space in relationships (or freedom from commitment). Sometimes the middle finger rests on the ring finger, suggesting duty dominates a desire for fun and creativity. A thumb held away from the hand demonstrates approachability, while when it's held very close to the palm it betrays a strong need for privacy or secrecy.

The Thumb A large thumb is one that is broad, solid and reaches at least halfway up the bottom section of the index finger. This reveals force of personality, determination and resolve. A small thumb (one appearing slight in comparison to the rest of the fingers) is a sign that you give up too easily or avoid taking positions of responsibility. If you have a small thumb, you must learn to accept challenges and see things through. In rare instances, you'll see a blunt, swollen-looking tip and a wide thumb nail. This is a 'clubbed thumb' and reveals intensity, perfectionism and an explosive temper, which is often hidden under a calm exterior.

The Index Finger When your index is longer than your ring finger, it shows a bossy personality in search of truth and self-understanding. At work, you are more interested in control and not losing sight of your ideals. When the index finger is shorter than the ring finger, it betrays an inner lack of self-confidence or a need to prove yourself to the world.

The Middle Finger When this finger stands head and shoulders above the ring and index, it shows a strong sense of morality, reserve and commitment. It may also be a sign that you need much time alone. When short (just a little longer than the ring or index), there is a big issue with society's rules and you may either decide to 'drop out' from the rat race or join an organisation that provides the structure you feel you lack.

The Ring Finger When longer than the index, there is a strong need to perform, express, show off, take risks, or work in a field that allows room for creativity. When short, there's a fear of taking risks. This is the sign of a very private person, and you may avoid public displays of affection or letting people know about your personal life.

The Little Finger When long (reaching halfway up the nail section of the ring finger), it shows you have a very persuasive way of speaking. (When crooked, it reveals shrewdness.) When short or slight-looking, you have a way with children because you still have a strongly childlike quality in yourself. Sometimes, you'll notice this finger is low-set (its base is a step down from the base of the other fingers). This can show a late developer who has a fear of intimacy due to difficulties with a parent being emotionally or physically absent.

The Palm Lines

After studying the general shape of the hands and fingers, your next step is to understand the major lines that sweep across the landscape of the palms. Lines represent your energy drives. The life line is your physical energy, the head line your mental and intellectual energy, the heart line your emotional energy, and the fate line the amount of energy you have to direct into work, responsibilities and ambitions.

Picture each palm line as symbolising a river. Studying its course, colour and depth will reveal both the strength and direction of the river's flow. A palm line that is broad and clear shows the river is strong and direct – indicating that you have a strong sense of purpose in that area. When a line is weak or feathery, the river's strength is less powerful and could easily dissipate – it warns of being half-hearted or negative in your approach.

An interrupted (broken) palm line indicates hesitancy or that a situation has forced you to stop and question the path you're travelling down. An uninterrupted line suggests that the 'energy' represented is free-flowing and can operate without obstacle.

When lines are very thick, it shows that you are pushing yourself too far, perhaps working too hard or expecting too much from your efforts. When palm lines are faint, however, it is as though you don't have the energy to provide a healthy balance in your life.

Palm lines have a twofold application. They reveal character traits that you have developed and they can also show events that played a part in triggering these personality traits.

EMPTY OR FULL PALM?

Another way that your palm communicates who you are is through the number of minor lines that accompany these four major lines. Look again at the palm print you have made of your hand. More lines on the hand suggest you respond greatly to people and situations in your life; you therefore tend to take on board more information as well as the feelings and anxieties of those around you. If you have palms full of many fine lines, you are hyper-sensitive and should avoid negative people who drain you. If you have only the major lines present, you are more self-protective but need to express your needs to avoid a build-up of stress. With fewer lines, you don't pick up atmospheres or other people's concerns so readily. You stay on track, attending to your own needs as well as the needs of those in – and beyond – your immediate circle.

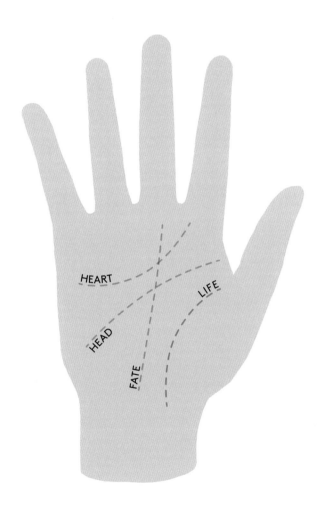

KEY TRAITS OF A FULL PALM	KEY TRAITS OF AN EMPTY PALM
★ Highly sensitive	★ Prefers to avoid deeply
★ Impressionable	emotional situations
★ Vulnerable	★ Steady
★ Intuitive	★ Sometimes labelled insensitive
★ An emotional sponge	to others
★ Potential for depression and	★ Inflexible
anxiety-related ailments	★ Has a black-and-white approach
★ Greater emotional resilience	★ Physically resilient and vigorous
than most	

WHAT IS YOUR DOMINANT HAND LINE?

Like your hand shape, the four major palm lines can be categorised by element. Sometimes one line is stronger than the rest, or perhaps one is more complex than the others. A few people have a Simian line (a joined head and heart line – see page 78), which will dominate the palm landscape.

STRONGEST AND WEAKEST LINES

If one particular line stands out, it is likely that what it represents dominates your life – how exactly it does this will be determined by the shape and course of the line. Sometimes all but one of the major lines appear to be of equal importance. If so, then that weakest line is in some ways your 'Achilles' heel', so take more notice of the profiles written about this line that are specific to your hand. On occasion, the standout line (whether the strongest or weakest) will differ from the left to the right hands, and the difference in meaning here should also be carefully considered.

DOMINANT LINE	ELEMENT	RELEVANT QUALITIES
Life	Fire	Enthusiasm, energy, challenge, physicality
Head	Air	Ideas, reasoning, questioning, communication, exchange
Heart	Water	Emotions, impressions, moods, perception
Fate	Earth	Practicalities, money, security, stability, routine

READING YOUR LINES

Where each of the major lines begins and where they terminate will tell you a great deal about your approach to life, your personality and your future. The depth, course, relative position and general appearance of the lines, plus any markings found on that line, link to events that occur in your life and your character traits. And each major line will describe your approach to work, love and life.

The profiles in the following sections offer more in-depth insight into what your lines can tell you.

The Life Line

DRIVE, PASSION & AMBITION

Are you one of life's bystanders or do you command the driving seat? Do difficulties send you off course or do they inspire you to travel into uncharted waters?

The life line tells us about the quality of your life, not your longevity. Understanding the course, strength and markings of your life line will reveal how much your determination to achieve and your sense of purpose steer your life.

Here, you can uncover clues to your physical and mental strength and health: the left hand's life line reveals your inherited health predispositions and your inner reserves of courage; while the right hand shows the extent of your stamina and drive in the outside world.

Do you have a short or missing life line? If so, you should strive to seek more passion and interest in your life. Or if parts of your life line are missing, you must learn how to weather the storm of change or ill health before you take on the world again.

Remember that the life line can fade out or strengthen over time, as well as develop additional strands, islands or branches. These developments 'coincide' with the changes you make to your inner (left hand) and outer (right hand) lives. For example, changing your diet or exercise routine will see a corresponding change in your hands.

Now, let's look at what the different positions and shapes of the life line mean on the following pages.

LOVE

Potential partners should beware: in pursuit of self-expression and a full life you demand a lot of time under the sheets! Sex is a basic and necessary outlet for your free-flowing physical energy, but remember to make the experience satisfying for all. You know better than most that a varied, fulfilling sex life will keep you youthful – partners will never be left in doubt as to whether you are still interested in them. When the base of your palm is wide, it suggests stamina and virility, making you an athlete in and out of the bedroom.

PERSONALITY

You understand that to succeed in any area of life you need discipline, determination and drive. You venture forth with confidence and tackle life head-on. For you, the secret of life is in the living – and you want to be living life to the full. When the thumb is strong, too, you give off an indomitable air of self-assurance, power and vitality. Others sense that with you around, things will be done thoroughly. They also know that you have little time for those who don't take chances or who moan about their woes.

WORK

Your life line won't dictate the kind of work you do, but a very strong line shows you thrive in environments that enable you to compete and get ahead. Others benefit if you take the role of group leader, but you prefer to focus on your own projects. A life line indicating good health could be put to good use in sports, outdoor activities, martial arts or weight training – anything that requires strong physical endurance, resilience and dedication.

The Leader

Strong Life Line

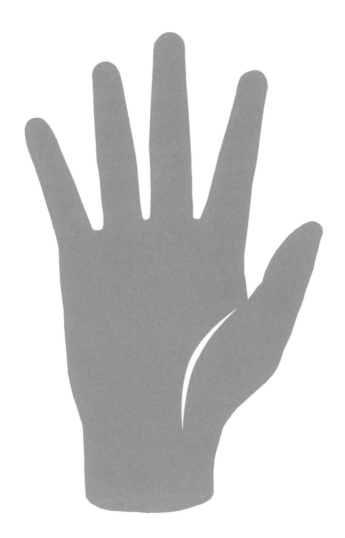

The Wallflower

Faint, Feathery Life Line

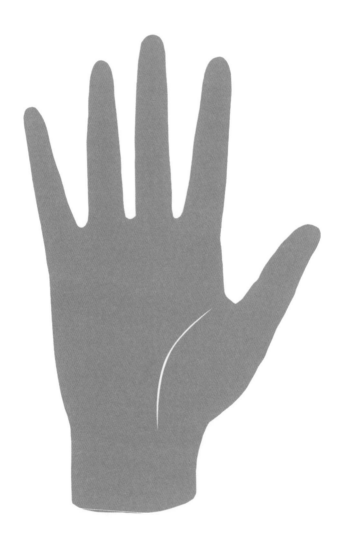

 ## LOVE

Sexually, a weak life line does not mean you won't have a fulfilling sex life, but it does suggest that other matters – such as anxieties and negative emotions – can get in the way. Depressive thoughts or frustration with life can subdue your enthusiasm for lovemaking. The most important point to remember is not to become lethargic or apathetic with your partner and in your sex life. At other times, though, you place sex too highly on your agenda, thinking that it compensates for feelings of inadequacy or insecurity.

 ## PERSONALITY

In general, you can be hesitant to push yourself out into the world. This is usually due to a psychological block, but sometimes it's down to a lack of confidence and timidity; at other times, it's indecision. It is important not to sideline yourself or think of yourself as a victim. Rather than just reacting to events, get out there and make things happen. Cultivate a stronger appetite for life. The key to living a fuller life lies in understanding yourself and giving yourself permission to make mistakes.

 ## WORK

Finding work that you can be passionate about is essential. Take more risks and have the courage to journey into the unknown. Don't look too far into the future, however. Instead, pour your energies into making a current project as fulfilling as possible. Move on when it ceases to be fruitful, or you will always be wondering if the grass is greener elsewhere. You may often avoid being in the driver's seat, but you would gain huge benefits from taking on a leadership role.

LOVE

This marking suggests an unrealistic tendency to expect every problem in a relationship to be resolved quickly. Without putting pressure on yourself to make major commitments, try to develop a long-term view of the relationship – it will help put matters in perspective. Fight the temptation to cut your losses and move on by channelling your efforts into cultivating long-lasting family relations and friendships.

PERSONALITY

Staying power may not be your strong point, but dedication and focus are invaluable traits to develop. Don't take the easy option when the going gets tough. Instead of believing in the adage 'all good things must come to an end', place trust in your own ability. When on the left hand only, a short life line is a sign that you feel detached from your family or ancestors. Perhaps your family moved around so often you felt rootless, or maybe situations at home seemed like they could change at any point, leaving you insecure about the future?

WORK

Your work often requires discipline and daily grind, but you can be resistant to this. Avoid jobs where you are swamped by emotions or forced to deal with heavy competition and gruelling deadlines, as you can be overwhelmed by too much responsibility. Short-term and project work are ideal. There may come a time when you want to slow down or stop altogether and have a lifestyle that is less stressful. With a short life line, anywhere away from the pressures of the rat race would suit you, preferably with a warm climate and relaxed attitudes.

The Drifter

Short Life Line

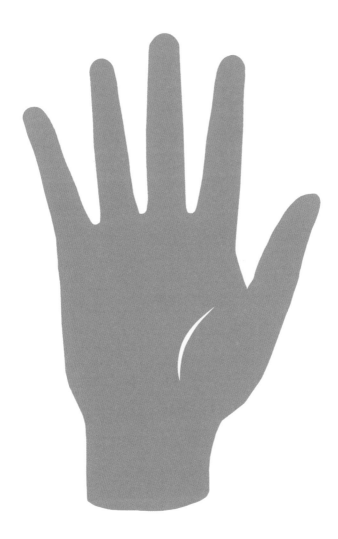

The Fighter

Two Equal Life Lines

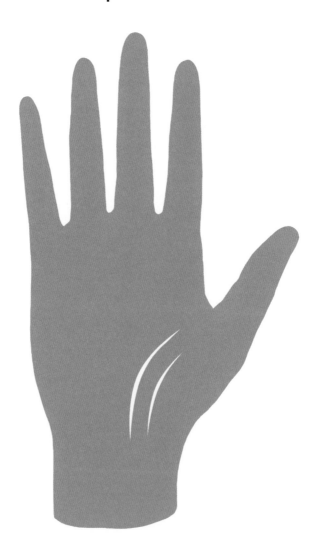

 # LOVE

You often carry more than your fair share of the emotional burdens of a relationship, and you may spend time looking after loved ones who do not have your strong recuperative powers. Partners respect your fighting spirit, but may object when your hot-tempered manner enters the emotional arena. They will experience your intensity first-hand, as well as a terse response when things don't go to plan. What people don't realise is you may lack confidence in personal relationships. You may have had to take responsibility from an early age and had less time for your own emotional development.

 # PERSONALITY

Even if the burdens from relationships or work sometimes get you down, you have a firmness and clarity of purpose that enable you to keep moving ahead. Your physical strength, resilience and never-say-die temperament see you win most of the confrontations in your life. Your forcefulness and fighting spirit ensure that you encounter more than most! You view life as hard work, but it is an uphill struggle that you are determined to win. Whatever your physical frame, there is a strength in your constitution that sees you fight off illness, fatigue and stress.

 # WORK

Two jobs, a handful of dependents, numerous responsibilities? No problem! You expect life to be a battle for financial survival and you are always ready to enter the fray. Your head line will suggest the type of work to which you are best suited, but with a double life line you should consider work that makes use of your physical strength and stamina.

The Change-Maker

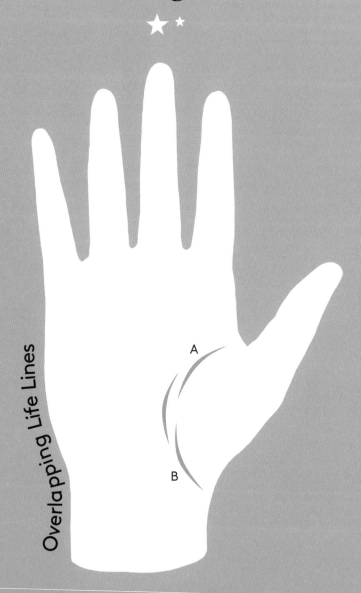

Sometimes two life lines appear on the hand, and often there is a distinct overlap between the old and new. This signifies a period of adjustment to a new lifestyle as old ties are slowly severed. The higher up on the hand, the sooner the transition occurs.

Arrangement A With this formation, an event or relationship causes you to venture forth on your own. You become more involved in the world and this new interaction forces you to re-evaluate the past and the person you are. This marking means that you could divide your life into two chapters: before and after self-discovery. It shows a change in attitude, where you take control of your life. Freedom accompanies this liberating, self-focused period.

Arrangement B This formation suggests a need to withdraw from the treadmill of the daily grind. It could be that difficulties have taken you away from your original plans. Your reaction may be to retreat to find peace of mind, but don't give up your dreams entirely. A change of focus is what is called for. Sometimes with this marking there is a shift towards the helping professions, and you may consider turning your talents towards one-to-one work.

This overlap is more likely to occur near the wrist, when there is a natural inclination to slow down. You may be advised to give up a hectic lifestyle, but it is vital not to become scared by life or over-protective of your health. Keep your sense of adventure. Take it easy but never consider retirement – always have a vocation or hobby.

A Sign of a New Beginning

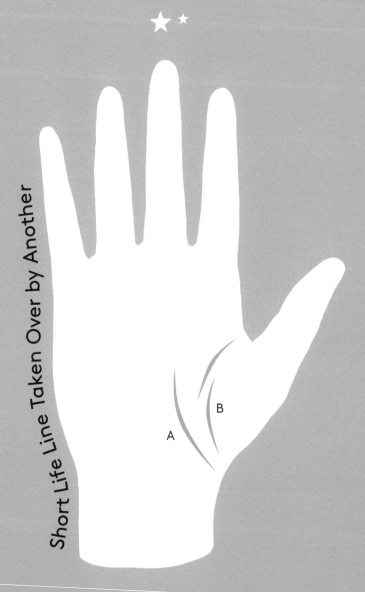

Short Life Line Taken Over by Another

A short life line that is substituted by another line does not signify a short life. The life line is often replaced by another line (usually another life line, the fate line or a Mars line) and these markings will help you determine the meaning.

The fate line takes over When the fate line takes over from the life line, it suggests an end to your routine or security. It implies there will be a need to begin again. Look on it as an opportunity for a new start. This shift often occurs in later years, when change is more challenging. Energy and stamina may be lacking (no life line) but duty calls and there are bills to be paid (the fate line takes over). It may be a time when you must summon up all your reserves of energy to start afresh. Sometimes it suggests you have been on automatic pilot personally (left hand) or professionally (right hand).

Another life line takes over When the life line is substituted by another life line originating from the wrist (see A), it is a sign of needing to turn your life around. It could be a change to your working or living environment, or it may be linked to a health decision.

The Mars line takes over If the Mars line (a shorter line that can form inside the life line) takes over from where the life line left off (see B), it is a sign of sheer willpower, a fighting spirit and strength of character. This means that, for you, the will to live is stronger than whatever ailments your body may face.

The Head Line

LOGIC, CREATIVITY
& MENTAL STRENGTH

Are you an intellectual, an entrepreneur or a creative type bursting with ideas? Do you prepare your plans and words carefully or simply shoot from the hip?

Perhaps the most revealing of all the lines, the head line reveals the extent to which you apply yourself to work, how efficiently you make decisions, how stress-prone you are, and how confident you are when articulating yourself. Professional success is often most clearly shown in the right-hand head line.

A delicate head line suggests your mental strength may be put under pressure, so be mindful of coming under too much stress. For example, you may need to accept you're not at your best in crises, or avoid jobs with punishing deadlines.

When the line appears heavy or coarse, your mode of self-expression – personally (the left hand) or socially/professionally (the right hand) – may lack finesse. Is your attitude or way of solving problems considered by others to be too blunt and bullish? Take time to consider how you are seen by others.

And if the line is woolly, faint or chained, it indicates a forgetful mind. Indecision is shown when the line breaks off into various strands at its end. If you have these markings, ensure you exercise your mind and your memory.

Compare your head lines on the left and right hands as they often differ quite markedly, revealing inconsistency between your private life and relationships (left) and your public and professional personas (right). Perhaps your confidence levels are markedly different, or in some ways you are two very different 'split' people.

LOVE

You look for equilibrium in all matters. You like to spend time exploring your feelings before making decisions. Partners may find it difficult to anticipate your moods or understand that you need time to process your feelings. You may have a tendency to be manipulative. When interested in someone new, you set out to win your prize. You'd benefit from expressing your true feelings rather than bottling them up or resorting to passive aggression.

PERSONALITY

You are perceptive, discerning and able to read between the lines. Combine this with a tactical approach and a readiness to deal hands-on with everyday matters, and you have the key palm sign of sound judgement. (If your head line is fuzzy or wavy, you need to work on staying focused, in order to be as productive with work and as clear-cut in your decision-making.) You also possess a temperament that questions everything. You'll need proof before you consider another's opinion as fact – and you need the facts before making a decision.

WORK

At your best, you have the cool, detached communication and reasoning skills that make you excellent in business. With this head line, you have the power to turn any creative talents to your financial advantage, particularly when in partnership with others. Your no-nonsense, practical approach, combined with a determination to tackle projects logically and with cunning, gives you good business acumen. In addition, you're great in a crisis because you are level-headed and rational.

The Decision Maker

Straight Head Line

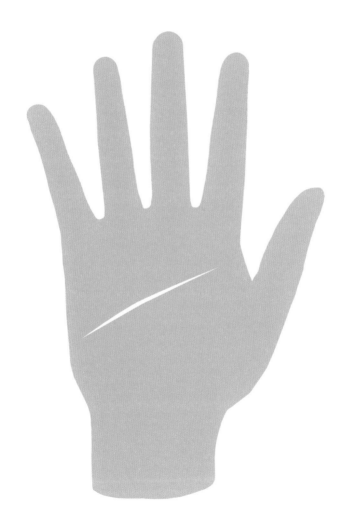

The Explorer

Curved Head Line

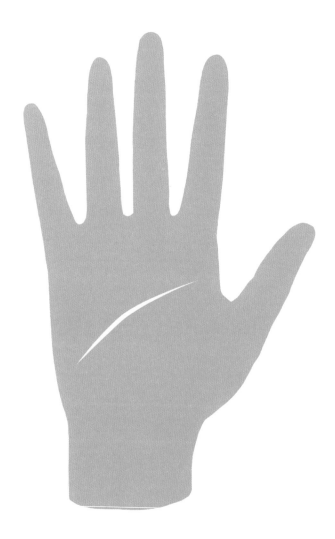

 ## LOVE

You love to surprise partners with presents and spontaneous gestures. You are open to exploring new ground sexually and dislike emotional games (particularly if your heart line is curved). You are just as candid when expressing your relationship needs. You are self-reliant and detached, and only share problems when you feel unable to cope on your own. Although not as practical as some, you would be just as happy to live on your own. Partners should respect your need for privacy and solitude.

 ## PERSONALITY

People know where they stand with you. You are open and expressive. You can sometimes take this too far, however, and can be tactless or undiplomatic. You are the type who wants to go with the flow, take calculated risks and explore new territory. For you, life is an adventure that could take a new twist any minute – and you want to be ready. You like things clear and simple and seek to find quick solutions to life's problems. You pursue life and all kinds of relationships with infectious enthusiasm.

 ## WORK

You seek to work for yourself or be in a company that offers opportunities to be autonomous. Yet straight-head-line counterparts may have an edge over you because you prefer not to play political games. You value the freedom to explore creative avenues over financial reward and security. You are motivated by the idea of producing a worthwhile end result, and would suffer in an ambitious environment where you have to watch your back. However, you do like to win respect and recognition for your creative versatility.

LOVE

First, look at the type of heart line you have, as this will tell you about your expectations and experiences in love (see pages 58–79). Your deeply curved head line suggests you are cautious in matters of the heart. Afraid of being vulnerable, you prefer the safety of your own secluded fantasy world. It's time to take stock, however. Anyone capable of penetrating your defences, particularly if you have creative pursuits in common, deserves to be given a chance. You have so much to offer, including a vast reserve of love and affection to share with others. But will you let them in?

PERSONALITY

You have enormous creative potential and a keen imagination, honed from an early age. Whether you were daydreaming at school or weaving intricate fantasies, you preferred to live in a world of make-believe. Now you'd rather avoid the harsh realities life throws your way, but don't run away from commitments. Find a way forwards without blaming others or avoiding responsibilities.

WORK

In school, your approach did not fit in with that of your peers. It's likely that you struggled with subjects that failed to spark your imagination. In later life, you may worry about not having the right qualifications. However, you are not best suited to highly competitive working environments. Resist the instinct to reject opportunities to express creative freedom for fear you won't be capable. Rise above the worry, trust your abilities and don't be afraid of success.

The Daydream Believer

Deeply Curved Head Line

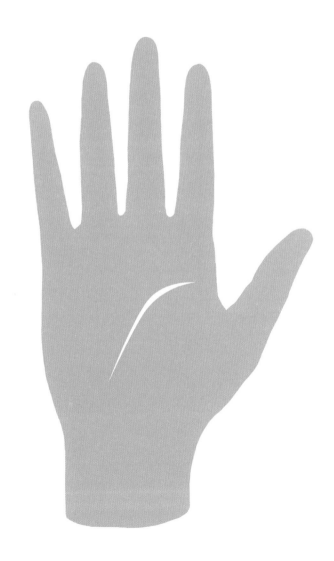

The Hot Head

Short Head Line

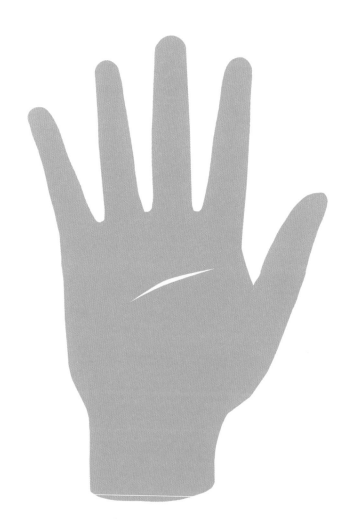

 **LOVE**

It is likely that your heart line is longer, meaning you are ruled by your heart, not your head. You are driven by your emotions and go with your gut reaction. You often don't think things through, preferring to duck out when the going gets tough. You also have a short fuse – only later are you able to process what's happened and digest the facts with objectivity. You hate complications, but create them when you act impetuously, often without thinking of the consequences.

 **PERSONALITY**

Your talent is to grasp the essence of an idea quickly. You have the sort of mind that can rapidly process the basic facts. You like to act incisively, and dislike complexities and red tape. Although making fast decisions (unless the head line is feathery or woolly) comes naturally, you may suffer if you don't 'do your homework'. You are at your best when you can apply yourself to a short-term situation. As an impulsive person, watch out for a tendency to bolt from situations when the pressure's on or when there are delays to your plans.

WORK

It is likely that you excelled in one or two subjects at school, and you may look at others and envy their versatility – but you are a specialist. You need work that requires a specific talent. Your mind works best when dealing with one project at a time – you tend to have a short attention span and you don't like distractions. You would excel as an authority in one area, and would do well in any job that requires handling money.

LOVE

You are a thinker who carefully considers the road ahead, but partners may not know where they stand because you tend to over-analyse relationship dilemmas. Will you stay or will you move on to new pastures? You don't make decisions until you have all the facts, but too much information may delay the process further. Nevertheless, partners need to come prepared if they start an argument with you – you are the type who will pull out a list of reasons why you are right.

PERSONALITY

You process information carefully, mulling over the details. One-to-one contact and talking things over with friends and colleagues is excellent therapy for you, as you depend upon feedback and two-way exchange. You hate to be pushed into making quick decisions – you fear missing a subtle but important point. Your thoughts flow most freely when there is no pressure. Being versatile, you have numerous interests and are able to handle many projects at once.

WORK

You have lots of ambitious plans but which one are you going to tackle first? It is important to organise your schedule and focus on long-term projects. A natural strategist, you have the patience to plan and see projects through. You know success comes from preparation and attention to detail. You may have a love of words and enjoy teaching and writing. As a student of life and probably well-read, you are able to bring a diverse range of experiences to any job you tackle.

The Thinker

Long Head Line

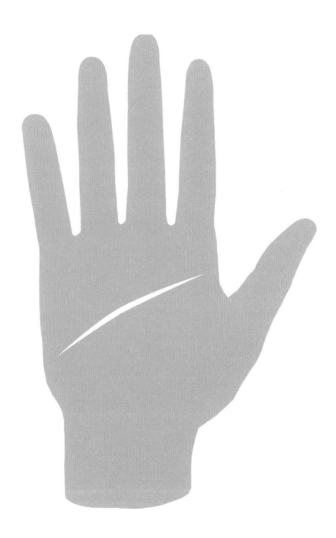

The Challenger

Head Line Starting Inside the Life Line

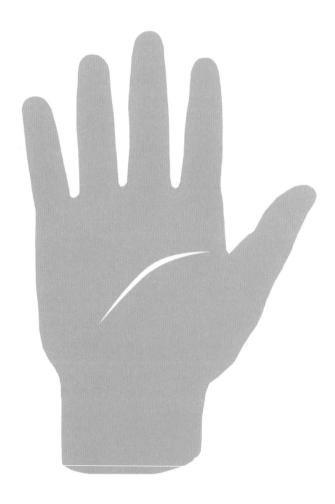

 ## LOVE

This can be a tough head line to have when in relationships. You are often rather tense and keyed up, so you find it difficult to relax with loved ones. Look to the shape and ending of the heart line (particularly on the left hand) to see how you can best express yourself emotionally. If friendships get in the way of personal plans, resist the impulse to cast them aside. Be mindful of your explosive temper and a tendency to be stubborn. Don't be reluctant to accept ideas and help from others.

 ## PERSONALITY

This head line gives you a personal style that is combative, but also courageous and dynamic. You are impatient and irritable but strong-willed and focused. You attack first and ask questions later. Subtlety is not your strong point. If you are determined to ride roughshod over the opposition, pay attention to your health, as you are stress-prone. Your hot-tempered approach to life can antagonise others. In fact, it may cause others to go out of their way to ensure you don't get what you want.

 ## WORK

You are not one to bother with fine details, particularly if you have short fingers or a short head line. However, you are excellent at getting to the heart of any matter and tackling problems head-on. Just be careful not to miss the subtleties. Others benefit from your no-nonsense, energetic approach. You will be considered an asset in any company that hires you to do battle, but you may need to take extended periods of time off work to unwind and disengage from stresses. If this is impossible, try to channel your aggression into sport instead.

LOVE

One of your greatest talents is your ability to charm others. You often seek out a partner who looks good on your arm but who won't have the charisma to outshine you. Your persuasive, self-confident manner attracts people, but sometimes your self-assurance is an act of bravado. Look for a partner who wants an equal relationship with you – this will curb your instinct to dominate or subjugate. However, you may struggle with a clash of wills if a loved one does not accept your opinion as gospel.

PERSONALITY

You have an imperious air of supreme confidence – some might call it cockiness. It is likely you had a healthy amount of encouragement when you were growing up, but this may have led to a tendency to be egocentric. You have big ambitions and set high goals for yourself. At best, you have an enterprising, generous and philanthropic nature. With a manner that commands respect, you have the potential to be influential and inspirational, but resist the urge to exert a Svengali-like control over followers.

WORK

It is likely that you had a desire at some stage to express yourself in one of the performing arts. You are suited to work that requires winning accounts and bringing in clients – work that makes full use of your ability to promote yourself or a product. Positions of authority are yours for the taking, but there may be times when your plans are thwarted because of your arrogance or a lack of training. You have many ambitions to succeed but must learn the ropes and some humility before you can earn your place at the top.

The Charmer

Head Line Starting
Near the Index Finger

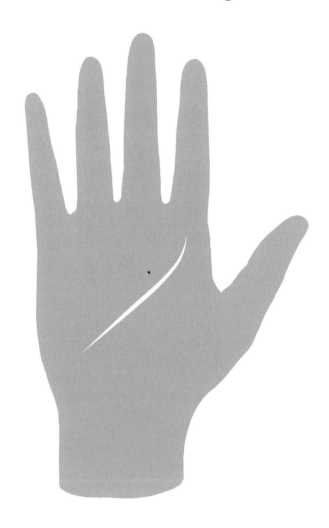

The Prodigy

Head Line with Additional Branch

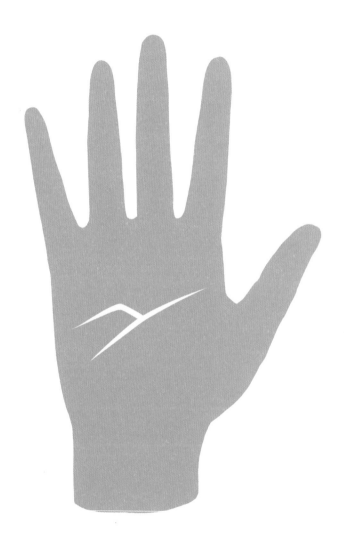

LOVE

With all your creative talent and potential for success professionally, your personal life may have its fair share of practical demands. You are ambitious and need a partner who also wants to push forwards, otherwise you will lose respect for them. You may be tempted to settle down with a steady, dependable partner, but ensure you choose someone who can also stimulate you intellectually, as you easily bore. Sometimes a partner feels they are taking second place to your many creative outlets – either work with them or adapt your hectic life to make room for a relationship.

PERSONALITY

You are gifted with mental dexterity and are driven to apply your ample creative talents. You will never be bored – for you, life offers endless choices. When the head line is curved, you express yourself in a dramatic way, such as performing or as a designer. It may be hard to earn a living from your talents because you need to learn to value yourself first. If the branch appears on a straight head line, though, you have learned to exercise your talents in a practical form.

WORK

You are highly adaptable, capable of processing fresh ideas and learning new subjects very quickly. Whether it is learning a language in six weeks or picking up a complicated dance move, you are able to grasp the essentials and apply them to your own goals. Others are amazed at how self-motivated, driven and ambitious you are. Aim to work in an area that brings you enormous pleasure.

LOVE

Often the more self-confident side of you is expressed through work, while the insecure worrier is revealed to those closest to you. Two head lines point to someone supremely capable in many areas of life but who can be demanding and immature in relationships. There is a gulf between how you perceive yourself in public and in private. Potential partners may be attracted to your enigmatic public image but may discover a different person behind closed doors. The key to happiness is in integrating both sides into your personal life.

PERSONALITY

Two head lines reveal a dual personality, each half struggling for dominance. Usually one of them begins near the index finger and seeps elegantly into the hand, while the other is tied to the life line and is much shorter. This suggests that one part of you is an outgoing, fun character that thrives on taking chances, starting new ventures and involving people in your life. The other is a withdrawn, sombre soul who can be distrustful and suspicious of others' motives. This combination can produce a neurotic personality that is intensely private yet driven to be out front, centre stage.

WORK

You are the ultimate promoter, publicist or fundraiser, and are keenly aware of how others see you. You are highly intelligent and very capable, if not slightly unpredictable. Colleagues will soon discover that the person who is articulate, confident and authoritative is also the person who, in private, is painfully shy and self-doubting. Some of you may even have a 'secret life' that few know about.

The Janus

Two Separate Head Lines

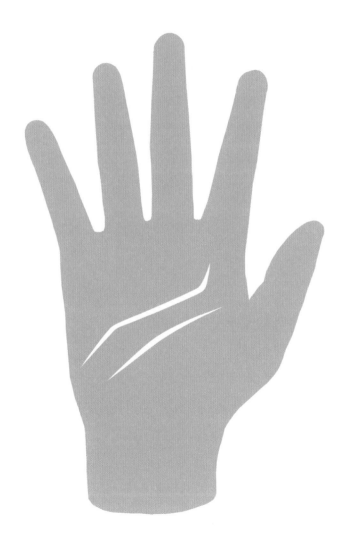

A Sign of a Big Change

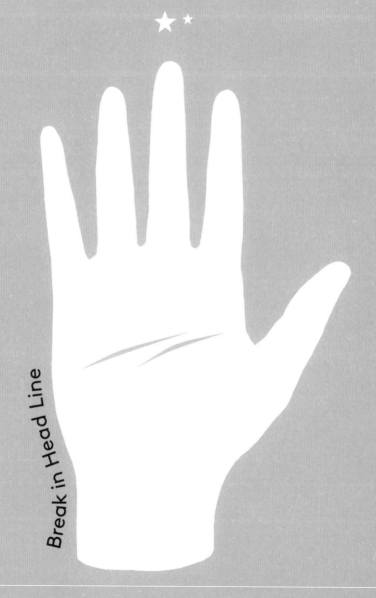

Break in Head Line

STARTING OVER

Breaks always signal the end of a chapter in your life. Look to determine whether the break is on the left hand (private self) or right (public self). When the first line stops, it signals an end to a way of thinking or behaving – often a definite break in routine or of a life path. Occasionally this could reflect a physical injury or shock, but often this change occurs because of a loss of some sort. It could be a loss of a relationship, through divorce, a parting of the ways, or the death of a loved one, or of an old self, symbolising being 'born again'. The strength and clarity of the new line will determine how strong and resilient this new path in life will be.

Sometimes the new line will emerge from the direction of the index finger, pointing to a new-found confidence in yourself, a spiritual rebirth or entering a position of greater control in your life. On other hands, the new line appears below the original. This implies that you have taken on an outlook that focuses on your inner self and you feel an impulse to withdraw from public life. Your main objective is to live your life for yourself rather than trying to please others around you.

OVERLAPS

Often the head lines will overlap and this shows a gradual acceptance of a change in routine, and a slow move towards a new life. Look to see whether the overlapping lines are protected by a square, suggesting the transition is smoother because of a constant in your life at that time. When the lines do not overlap, a break away from recent stresses must be made in order to take stock and regroup.

The Heart Line

LOVE, SEX & RELATIONSHIPS

The heart line (or love line) is the prime indicator of your emotional and sexual make-up. It describes how you begin and end relationships, how you tackle emotional and sexual problems, and the type of problems you have in partnerships, both sexual or platonic. Essentially, it reveals how you relate to others on an emotional level. Does your heart rule your head? It may do, if the heart line is longer or deeper than the head line on the left hand. When longer on the right hand, you may 'wear your heart on your sleeve' and emotions may strongly influence your decisions.

Most heart lines begin with a short series of interwoven lines, resembling a chain of small links. In addition to this, they often feature branches, island formations and crossing lines. This suggests a normal and healthy measure of emotion and vulnerability. The heart line usually ends in a small fork underneath the index and middle fingers, which demonstrates a balance between realism (middle finger) and idealism (index finger) in relationships and the need for honest and regular communication.

There are two further general points to remember when examining the shape of the heart line: a complex-looking heart line demonstrates an equally complex set of emotional-sexual responses, while an unmarked or evenly laid out heart line suggests emotional coolness or a difficulty in feeling empathy or passion.

Occasionally the heart line is missing, and more often than not this is due to the presence of a Simian line (see page 78). Sometimes there appears to be a doubling-up of the heart line. When this happens, the heart line takes on enormous importance and both lines should be assessed carefully.

LOVE

Others may accuse you of looking at life through rose-tinted glasses, but you are simply an idealist. You know that settling for second best is tantamount to defeat. You swing from feeling that your relationship works well to wondering why there seems to be 'something missing'. In fact, your expectations are sometimes too high – don't expect partners to be superhuman psychics. They can't always know what you want or be able to fill the voids you have. Work on investing in yourself rather than looking for a partner to reinforce these feelings.

PERSONALITY

You are demonstrative and warm, able to put people at ease and make them feel like the most important person in the room. Yet giving 100 per cent of yourself to others sets you up for disappointment when most don't reciprocate as fully. You tend to put friends, family and lovers on a pedestal and are genuinely hurt when they fall off – you forget that they are human and most are not as generous with time and money as you are. Perhaps you do so much for others because you yearn for the same in return?

WORK

You are a generous colleague and the first to offer workmates a shoulder to cry on. Your positive, spontaneous nature and optimism can inspire others in work and in love, and you could find a professional role to this end (as long as you know you can only inspire others, not change them). You work hard to win friends by being generous, but can feel rejected when you realise that many colleagues won't go the distance for you. Your toughest challenge is to give without the expectation of anything in return.

The Idealist

Curved Heart Line to Index Finger

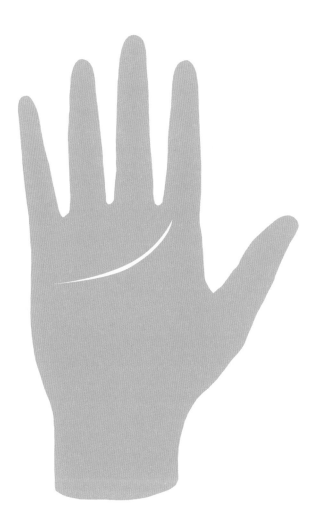

The Pleasure-Seeker

Curved Heart Line to Middle Finger

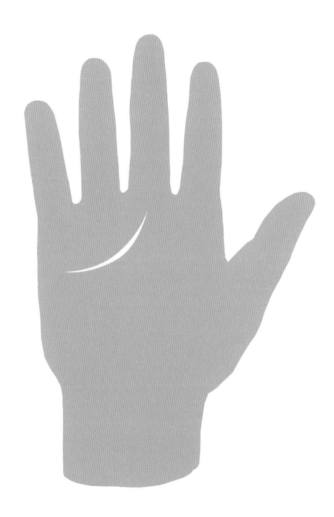

 ## LOVE

Yours is a strong sexual nature, interested in extremes. You enjoy the chase, the sparks of sexual chemistry and the pursuit of pleasure. Partners may be intimidated by your intensity and insatiable need to experience everything physically. At the same time, they may feel you are 'unreal' because you never let your emotional guard down. You have learned to avert their interest in the real you by attracting them sexually. But an emotionally satisfying union will require trust; you'll need to risk exposure by revealing the person behind the façade.

 ## PERSONALITY

Who are you? Are you really the person that everyone around you encounters, or is it just an act? You fear that if you drop your mask, others will see your faults that seem so apparent to you. This mask is also a form of self-protection to avoid being hurt by something you were not able to protect yourself against when younger. Putting up a brick wall keeps out those wanting to pry into your soul. This heart line formation suggests a quest to reinvent yourself and you may try on various masks along the way to see which fits best.

 ## WORK

You may be attracted to work that requires you to play a role that is very different from your true self. Or perhaps playing someone else helps you understand your real personality. The obvious choice may be acting, where you can draw from your experiences but project a different character to an audience. You may, though, resist the exposure and soul-bearing demanded by acting and feel drawn to professional situations in which you can hide behind a front, or be anonymous.

LOVE

You tend to be very analytical and often spend time questioning your feelings and those of your partner. A lover can't make any comment without it being processed and analysed. A good judge of character, you nevertheless tend to be a harsh critic. You look for many signals from a prospective partner before committing yourself, and you have a mental checklist of characteristics they must have to qualify. Having dissected and investigated a situation, you can sometimes be afraid to express yourself. You should avoid suffering in silence or playing emotional games. When there are problems, learn to tackle them head-on and express your needs and desires clearly.

PERSONALITY

In life, you balance idealism with a practical approach to personal and professional commitments. Although you want to believe the best of everyone, you accept that relationships of all kinds require nurturing, support and hard work. You have a mature, long-term view of life – so it will come as no surprise that you value reliability and honesty in others, and honour the commitments you make personally.

WORK

As dedicated in your work as you are to personal commitments, you strike a good balance between practical application and hopeful optimism. You are a valuable ally and a dependable support system for colleagues. Yet why are you sometimes overlooked for promotion? You are shrewd and considered in your approach, but you are not so good at asking for things for yourself. Make sure that you focus on your own professional needs, too!

The Over-Thinker

Straight Heart Line Ending
Below Index Finger

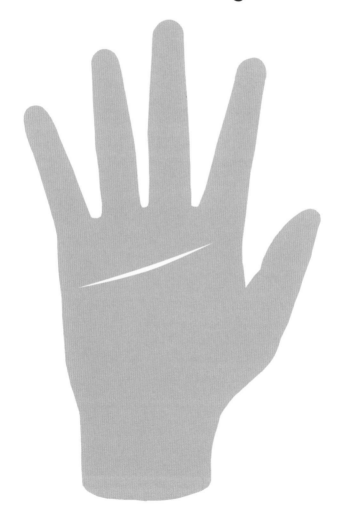

The Cynic

Straight Short Heart Line

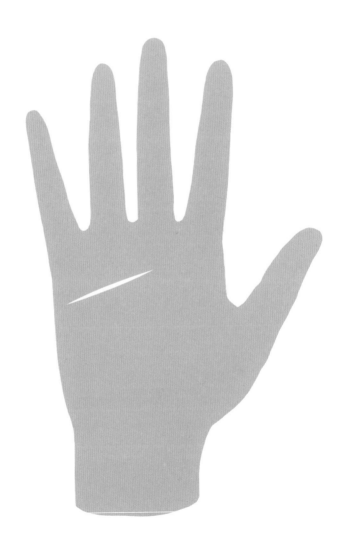

LOVE

Will sex lead to love? Although you may find yourself seeking sexual contact to form a bond, deep down you would prefer to do this through expressing your emotions. But you are afraid to expose your vulnerability. You find it easier to operate on a purely sexual level and hope that this will fulfil your needs, but you'll find it more rewarding to explore emotional depths with a loved one capable of doing this. Be more open and honest, and let a sexual union stem from a meeting of minds. Forget being a pragmatist and have the courage to dive in at the deep end.

PERSONALITY

Forgetting the past is harder for you than most. Your cynical attitude to life may be justified, but it does you little good. Past hurts resurface when you find yourself attracted to someone new – your instinct is to protect yourself by hiding beneath a tough, caustic armour. Or perhaps you are so focused on having your own needs met that you neglect your partner's? Either of these responses provokes the negative response you were expecting. Try to work these through. Don't seek love and friendship by courting rejection.

WORK

This challenging heart line faces potential difficulties in the workplace, too. A sensitive soul like you can sometimes fall victim to office politics because your instinct is to reveal too much of yourself to win friends. You may find that clamming up not only protects your position but also gives you control over your environment. Try helping others, maybe as a counsellor or advisor, as you can then empathise with them while healing your own wounds.

LOVE

You have the ability to connect on a deeper level than most people. Yet this intensity can scare those who are afraid of exploring their intimate feelings. However much you work at it, some partners will be unwilling or unable to do this. So at times you may have been hurt by someone who did not commit with the same intensity. A painful lesson, but a mourning for what you have shared will be met with an acute realisation of what was missing. When relationships end, it is not uncommon to have negative or self-destructive thoughts. Be mindful of becoming depressed or even obsessed. Recognise the limitations of others and move on.

PERSONALITY

Most people are sensitive souls but often insensitive to the feelings of others. You, however, are highly sensitive but can also empathise and offer support. Your early experiences have made you delicate when it comes to rejection, but they have also given you the tools to help others gain understanding. Avoid cutting yourself off from the hurt of rejection by refusing to trust again. Remember that life will always be richer for having dared to love.

WORK

Your compassionate nature makes you a natural in the helping professions. Counselling, support groups or an advice board would benefit from your understanding of grief and loss. But remember: you can only be of genuine help if you have worked on your own feelings and moved on.

The Confidant

Heart Line Descending into the Life Line

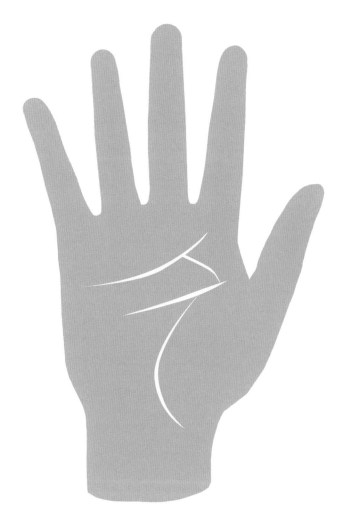

Introvert or Extrovert?

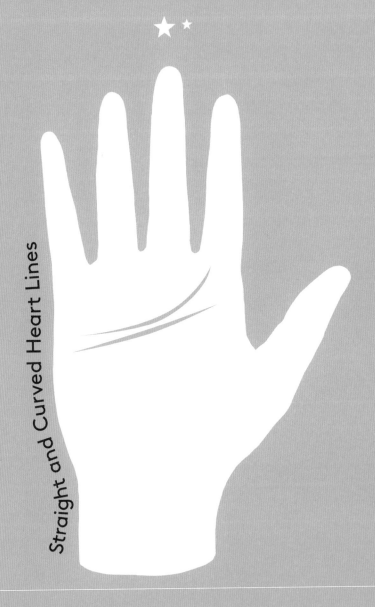

Look at the shape of the heart line. Does it run straight across the palm? Does it curve deeply towards the fingers? The shape of the line reveals inward and outward expressions of emotion, and the way you relate to others in a partnership.

COMMON TRAITS OF THOSE WITH A STRAIGHTER HEART LINE:	COMMON TRAITS OF THOSE WITH A MORE CURVED HEART LINE:
★ Emotionally reserved, even introverted	★ Emotionally demonstrative, extroverted
★ Controlled, thoughtful and analytical	★ Spontaneous and enthusiastic
★ Looking for sincere, earnest long-term mates	★ Looking for attractive, daring mates
★ Seeking emotional and mental compatibility	★ Seeking physical and sexual chemistry
★ Likely to wait for signs of interest	★ Happy to initiate contact
★ Seeking equality and a supportive union	★ Wanting to conquer, dominate and win
★ Expressive via words and memories	★ Expressive via presents and surprises
★ Uses sex to bond, unite and reassure	★ Uses sex to empower and release tension
★ Sometimes inhibited and afraid to ask	★ Often exhibitionistic and can want too much
★ Adverse to discord, tension or unpredictability	★ Dislikes stale or predictable situations
	★ Hot-tempered – quits the relationship then makes up

Empathetic or Self-Involved?

★ ★

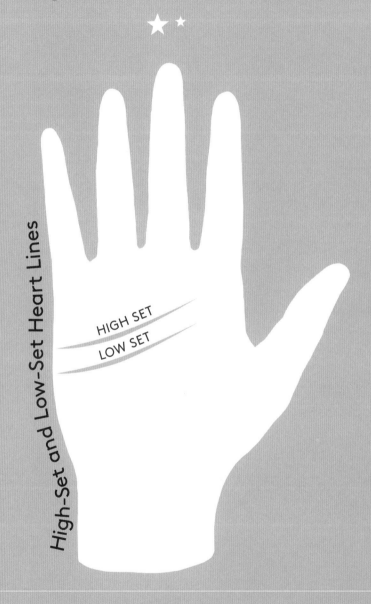

High-Set and Low-Set Heart Lines

HIGH SET

LOW SET

Most heart lines are set a good distance from the base of the fingers, but sometimes the line is either higher up or set significantly lower, nearer the head line.

HIGH-SET

Often you are too wrapped up in yourself to empathise with someone else. If you do find time to listen, your response is to compare it to one of your own experiences. You may fall into the category of the incessant head-nodder – the type you often see interviewing people on TV who is too busy mentally preparing the next question and not listening. Or maybe you're the type who can top any tale of woe with your own personal story. When your index finger is long, you put yourself in the other person's place long enough to give them advice on how to run their lives. Everything would be fine if they would follow your suggestions! With a long ring finger, though, you would like to be seen to help, but you would really rather get off the phone and call someone who wants to hear about you instead.

LOW-SET

You make a very good listener and can relate to others' problems and offer support. In this case, the heart line is closer to the head line, suggesting an ability to provide constructive feedback. Although focused on your own life, you are able to help others by drawing on your experiences. If your index finger is long, you empathise but want to see proof that they are picking themselves up. You are a firm believer in encouraging others to be self-determining and have no time for self-pity. If the ring finger is dominant, you will let them wallow and be happy to throw in a few of your own hard-luck stories.

Islands, Arrows & Branches

★ ★

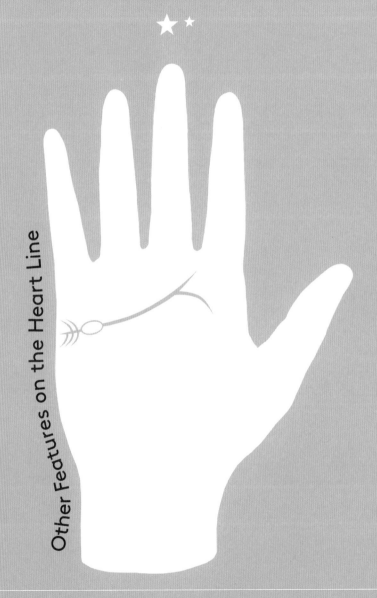

Other Features on the Heart Line

ISLANDS IN THE HEART LINE

These show the changes you must make during relationships. There are usually fewer islands later in the heart line, suggesting you grow more comfortable with yourself with age. The fact that so many palms have major islands in the heart line suggests that relationships can often bring out insecurities and force you to work hard to keep the union strong. A long island that follows a sloping branch off the heart line shows difficulties adjusting after the break-up of a relationship. (All short, sloping branch lines at the early to middle stages of the heart line show difficulties or endings.)

ARROWS AT THE START OF THE HEART LINE

These marks are signs of jealousy – not just the green-eyed type but, at worst, the more unpleasant, spiky, sharp-tongued, resentful sort. You may be notoriously self-protective, too. You should recognise a destructive side in you that is unforgiving and unwilling (or unable) to put aside past hurts.

A DESCENDING, HOOK-LIKE BRANCH

This marking, which does not touch the life or head line, shows that there was a difficulty in understanding your sexuality in adolescence. Perhaps there was confusion around your own sexual feelings or perceptions. When found on the left hand, this is a deep-rooted concern. It suggests doubt over your sexual identity and desires, whatever your orientation. If found only on the left, these doubts may remain private. When only on the right, you may benefit from exploring your feelings in the open with like-minded people.

Open-Minded or Narrow-Minded?

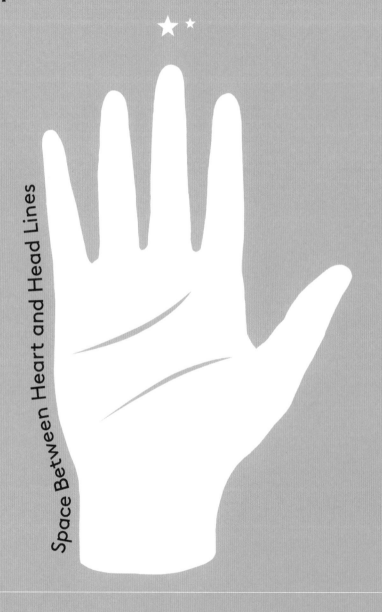

Space Between Heart and Head Lines

Any connection between the heart and head lines tells us something about the link between emotional needs (heart) and mental approach (head).

The space between these lines reveals how you separate your emotional instincts from intellectual reactions. Are you detached and objective, or involved both emotionally and mentally? (A branch linking these lines suggests that relationships will suffer unless there are efforts to develop clear lines of communication.)

People with an average or unremarkable space between these lines are usually open to others but make decisions based upon their own belief systems, too.

A WIDE SPACE BETWEEN THE LINES INDICATES THAT YOU ARE:	A NARROW SPACE BETWEEN THE LINES INDICATES THAT YOU ARE:
★ Broadminded and open to suggestion and influence	★ Quite narrow-minded, inhibited, unswayed
★ Tolerant, liberal, 'live and let live'	★ Often influenced by moral/ religious codes
★ Generally unprejudiced, impartial	★ Focused, controlled, dedicated
★ Able to separate thoughts from feelings	★ Able to make decisions with head and heart

Those with a Simian line (see page 78) will share many traits of those who possess a narrow space, but these characteristics will be more intensified and will dominate their character.

The Simian Line

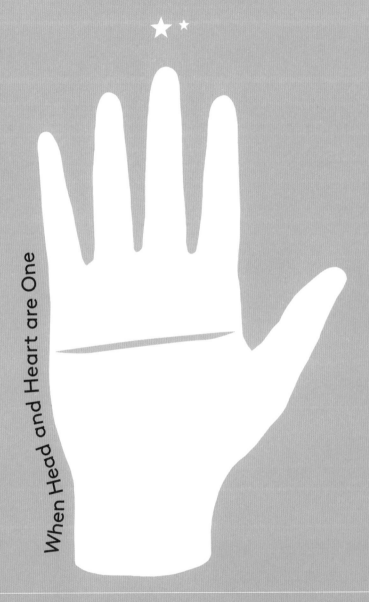

When Head and Heart are One

One of the most fascinating marks on the hand, the Simian line indicates intensity and personality extremes. Instead of having separate head and heart lines, the Simian line is one strong line travelling across the palm like a single railway track. If you have this, it suggests a one-track mind and a propensity for tunnel vision. You are focused, intense and volatile in your personal style.

The Simian line is usually present on one hand only. On the left hand, it relates to personal relationships and feelings, and may suggest a chaotic personal life. You may have trouble feeling 'at peace' in private, never being able to relax and switch off. You are always searching for a way to express yourself. Partners can be driven away by your need to possess, control and dictate their every move. When found only on the right hand, it is expressed in the outer life and working environment, which can be equally chaotic without a balanced rhythm or something on which to focus. When the line appears on both hands, the characteristics of a Simian line are greatly intensified.

This line creates extremes in personality and there is little middle ground, so it is not at all uncommon to find that you function brilliantly in one area of your life but are completely unable to cope in another. One of the main themes of the Simian line is control. Traditional palmists often associated this marking with violence, aggression and brutality. However, some modern palmists see this line as heralding great success, particularly when found on the right hand or both hands. The Simian line dominates the hand to such an extent that you can either be a runaway success, capable of great originality, or a misguided, self-destructive missile.

With this line, the accompanying elements essential for a balanced life are strong thumbs and long fingers, which add willpower, reasoning, attention to detail, and diplomacy into the mix. With these features, you become a 'triple threat', able to win over others through charm and leadership ability. Supremely focused and disciplined, you are a force to be reckoned with.

The Fate Line

WHERE ARE YOU GOING IN LIFE?

Where are you going in life? What drives you to succeed? What is your attitude to work and what does success mean to you? The fate line depicts your goals, your view of responsibility and commitment. It shows how you interact with your environment and the routines you have built up at work and in close relationships.

This is the most fascinating line of all, as its length, direction and course all provide clues as to your life path, aims and ambitions – as well as the extent to which you can shape your future. By understanding the fate line, you can unravel the dramas in your life: the fascinating twists and turns of fate and the influential people you encounter along the way.

Your fate line can tell you whether you want the security of employed work or prefer freelance independence, whether you are motivated by money or driven by high-flying ambitions, married to your work or desperate to break away from the family firm. Looking at the fate line is likely to add huge value to your life.

Absent fate line This shows that you refuse to 'play the game', preferring to live life on your own terms. You may be unable or unwilling to settle down into a routine. At best, you may have an unconventional approach to life, accompanied by a keen interest in various ideas and pursuits. At worst, it can indicate that you drift aimlessly or are unable to commit personally (left hand) or professionally (right hand). There may be an accompanying rejection of societal or parental expectations.

Missing in part If your fate line is missing in places, this indicates a period when a career or life path is lacking in direction. If the fate line begins higher up in the hand, there may have been work and routine earlier but nothing that was personally satisfying or rewarding. When the line finally takes shape, this is an indication of you finding your niche or settling down into a steady, secure routine. Remember that the fate line can change course, fade out or strengthen over time as you respond to the changes you make to your inner and outer environments.

LOVE

When you commit, it is rare that you change track in love. In fact, you make commitments seriously and with sincerity. You will choose someone with a view to sharing your long-term future. You want a life partner who is focused and not put off by temporary relationship difficulties. Watch out for the tendency to put work before love, though. Steady and committed, others may find you somewhat predictable and rather conservative in your day-to-day routine, but at least they will know what to expect!

PERSONALITY

You do things your own way and tackle life systematically. Your work ethic and sense of responsibility come from your family. You are tough on yourself: a control freak who imposes a strict code of conduct. If others accuse you of being dull, you know that common sense spells success. Risk-taking is for others; you prefer the steady climb, but could benefit from taking risks when opportunities come your way.

WORK

You have a conscientious and reliable approach to work. You pride yourself on reaching goals and love a job done well, whether it is housekeeping or running a company. You set clear, attainable targets and work towards them, often thinking about work in terms of a career rather than a job. Your ability to plan is one of your strengths. Taking the occasional risk, though, will mean you won't stagnate or miss opportunities to stretch yourself and develop your talents.

The Stalwart

Strong Unbroken Fate Line

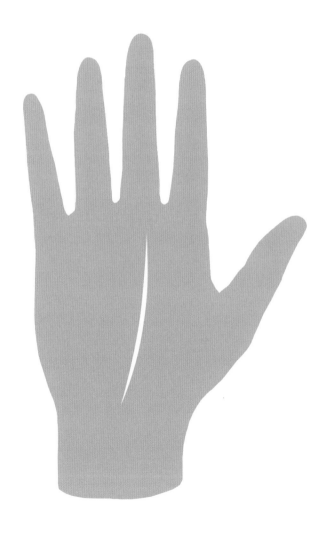

The Rolling Stone

Fine, Faint or Feathery Fate Line

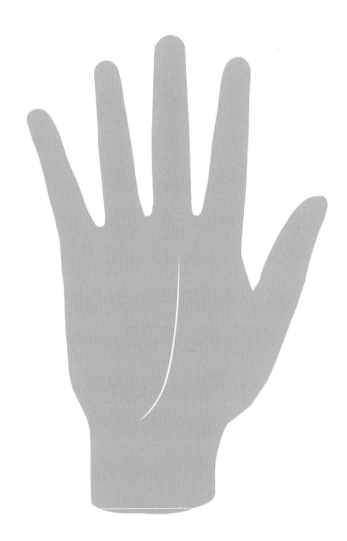

 ## LOVE

Relationship issues dominate your life and this leaves little time to develop work that is satisfying and self-expressive. Don't abandon your creative needs or your independence if someone offers to take care of you. Until you find a healthy balance you may resist partnerships that demand long-term commitment. Drifting along until it becomes unbearable means you are taking part but not playing a leading role. Your greatest achievement will be learning how to live in the moment while developing relationships and pursuing fulfilling work.

 ## PERSONALITY

If life feels unpredictable, it is not surprising that you might fear the future and look for quick ways to feel secure and settle down. Just be careful not to settle for second best. Perhaps you also need to accept that you don't care much for responsibility. Rather than taking on duties and later running away from them, decide to have a more carefree existence with fewer obligations. You should, however, aim to make your daily life as full as possible – just avoid attracting unnecessary stress or hassle.

WORK

It is important to find work that makes use of your talents. You may prefer to opt for a non-competitive life – but you sometimes put pressure on yourself to succeed on others' terms. Be assured, you will create a fulfilling and unique life for yourself when you accept your own ideas of success. Your heart needs to be in your work, otherwise you may become lethargic and unreliable. Negative thinking is a waste of your abilities. Find a passion to be passionate about.

LOVE

At times, it seems as though you are forced to choose between work and romantic commitments, when, in fact, you have the discipline and energy to handle both successfully. Partners may be openly resentful of the time you give to other aspects of your life. Rather than asking you to choose, they should be proud of your ability to attend to commitments inside and outside the home. They also need to realise that, for you, a relationship is like a full-time job. You seek out good prospects, assess the long-term potential, and work consistently to get results.

PERSONALITY

This interesting feature shows versatility and the capacity for hard work. Although it may seem that you juggle responsibilities endlessly, you do take all aspects of your life seriously and display enormous focus and commitment. Make sure you have time to relax, travel and recharge your batteries.

WORK

A double fate line could suggest two jobs, or at least imply that there are two avenues to which you dedicate your time. Often it is juggling a demanding career and a busy home life, but the result could be that you don't give yourself enough pampering or 'downtime'. Sometimes with a double fate line, lovers are business partners working alongside you or are in some way involved in your professional life.

The Juggler

Double Fate Line

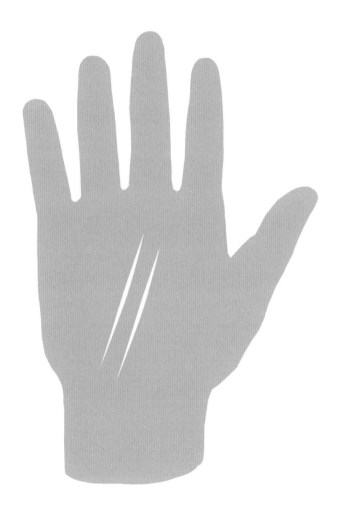

The Vagabond
Numerous Fate Lines

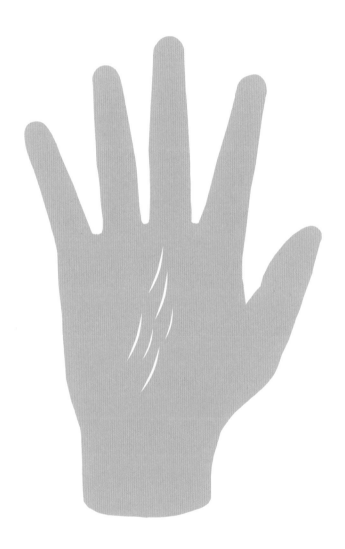

 ## LOVE

There is a side to you that believes that relationships are transient; that friends come and go and there are few lasting ties. At worst, you may use others as stepping stones, leaving behind a trail of hurt, resentful people. You may enjoy a footloose time or a period of serial monogamy, but don't lose track of the important 'constants' in your life. Cultivate trust by being there for those who share your approach to life, and consider seeking a life of variety with one person in particular.

 ## PERSONALITY

You may have developed a reputation for indecision and an inability to see things through, but on the plus side you thrive on change, and can be sparkling company. You have a low boredom threshold – there is always something else that promises to be more appealing. It is likely that your life will be filled with many interests; you are keen to try out various lifestyles or jobs before you settle down. Others shouldn't worry too much about you – when one door threatens to close, you will always have a foot in the next room.

 ## WORK

You would do well in the media or any job that requires versatility. Rather than arranging a long-term career plan, go with the flow and try your hand at various things. Recognise that change is inevitable and that you need a varied life with few restrictions. See what suits you at any point in time and pour your energies into making it a success. Long-term plans with little room for adjustment are not for you. If you insist on having a long-term plan, you will have to develop greater initiative, drive and staying power.

LOVE

Partners may have to contend with your preconceptions about relationships. You may be prone to making unfair comparisons between them and your family or past lovers. Early unions may have suffered because you were tied to beliefs ingrained in childhood, or perhaps you had to contend with family opposition and interference. Did you commit too early because you felt it was 'the thing to do'? You will have your most successful relationships when you have drawn clear boundaries between you and your family. Take time to learn what it is that you want. If commitment comes a little later in life, it will be accompanied by a mature approach that benefits you both.

PERSONALITY

After feeling held back by family or responsible for their welfare, you have needed to develop a strong sense of who you are to succeed. Breaking away from these early restrictions will leave you more certain of your strengths and limitations. Remember that fighting your way out of a situation has made you stronger. You are not a time-waster. Draw strength from the motto 'better late than never'.

WORK

Don't worry if it has taken longer for you to find your true vocation. You haven't missed the boat, your early years were good preparation for what you can now offer. You have learned valuable lessons and are more realistic about what you can expect from others. Even if you stay with the family business, this later surge of working success will be on your own terms. You are a self-made person and you can thank yourself for getting to where you are today.

The Late Bloomer

Fate Line Beginning Halfway Up the Life Line

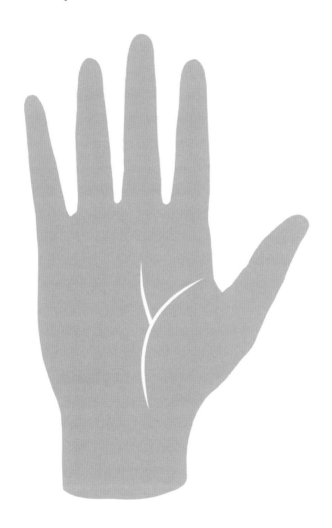

The Dependable One

Fate Line Starting from the Base of the Life Line

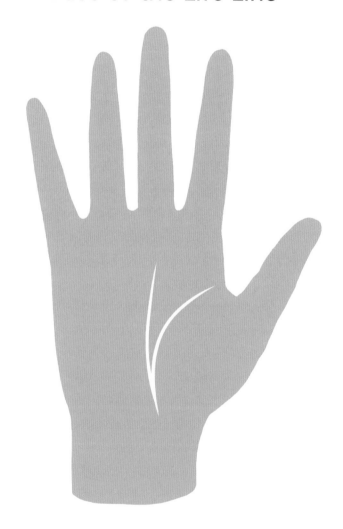

 ## LOVE

You might find it difficult to assert your independence in love, as family demands can get in the way. How can partners be as committed to you as you are to your family? By judging lovers in this way, you are doing them a disservice. In fact, it is likely that you are attracted to their independence and refusal to let others rely too heavily on them. The right relationships will, at some stage, force you to assert your own independence and help you build a healthy distance from your family.

 ## PERSONALITY

You carry the burdens of others on your own shoulders. You have taken the role of the dependable person, and others can take advantage. They see you are co-dependent and some may use emotional blackmail to keep you at their beck and call. However much you display independence elsewhere, with family there appears to be a strong tie of dependence that you allow to remain, often to your cost. On the positive side, you cherish the family unit and seek security by wanting your own family.

 ## WORK

You show strong dedication and could follow a path in the service or nursing professions. When this formation occurs on both hands, it suggests you felt your family demanded much from you as you grew up, and you carry a sense of obligation to them. Perhaps when you began working you were required to put money back into the family home or much of your spare time was taken up with family business. For some (especially when on the right hand), your need to support the family (or a fear of making it on your own) saw you follow in the family's footsteps.

LOVE

Friends and lovers may come and go as your life and interests take you to new places. You seek variety and stimulation in love and friendship. Those unable to move with you will be left behind. Those willing to stay on board will find that you open up a world of new ideas, and widen their network of friends. Often partnerships arise out of friendship or shared interests. You may find love takes you to another country and requires you to learn a new language or set of customs, or embrace another religion.

PERSONALITY

So many places, faces and names to remember! You want your life to be full of eclectic experiences, encounters and escapades. Your personality is able to tap into what other people want. Sensing their concerns and anticipating their needs makes you able to put people at ease. You are adaptable enough to be an agreeable, pleasant person who is all things to all people. Your innate friendliness stems from a need to please and from having felt an outsider at some stage.

WORK

This is one palm sign that reveals a born communicator, someone who wants to be directly involved in interacting with the public. You strive to express yourself. Where other signs reinforce this, you look for a career that serves the public's needs and tastes (from running a venue to performing on stage). You are in tune with popular trends and have your finger firmly on the zeitgeist. Work opportunities are sporadic, so you must learn to pursue project or freelance work. Seek openings by making use of your various social and professional contacts.

The Born Adventurer

Fate Line Starting from the Outer Edge of the Palm

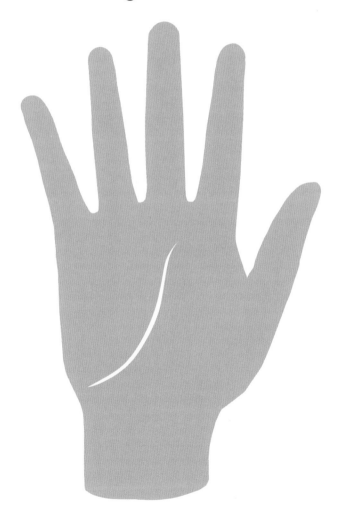

Three Signs of Success

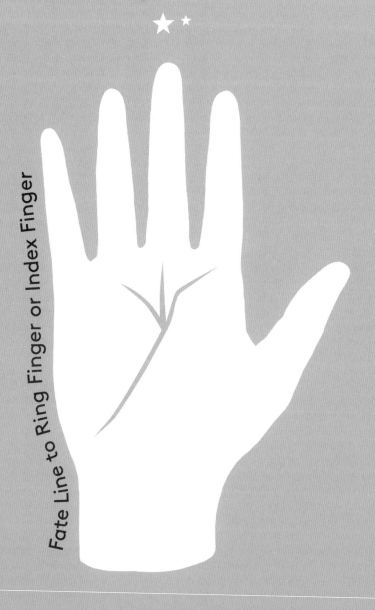

Fate Line to Ring Finger or Index Finger

Where the fate line ends gives a strong indication of where you will end up and the type of success your hard work will bring you.

ENDING UNDER MIDDLE FINGER

Most fate lines end on the Saturn mount, a centimetre or two under the middle finger. This indicates that you have worked hard and followed the natural process of slowing down. If various strands of the fate line begin at this stage, this shows that you take up a number of interesting pursuits but may not have enough energy to carry them all out. Be selective and avoid dispersing your energy. When the accompanying lines begin further down, it is known as the 'ladder of success', and has been seen on palms of self-made people who have reached the top through persistence and dedication. If the main fate line extends all the way to the base of the middle finger, you resist retirement and refuse to slow down.

ENDING UNDER RING FINGER

Your creative approach to work will ensure recognition and respect – sometimes more easily than you expected. You will have a good measure of fame and acclaim. Most of all you seek work through which you can express and enjoy yourself. Check the hand shape, the head line and the dominant fingers to see where this success occurs.

ENDING UNDER INDEX FINGER

This is a highly auspicious sign. Your work, leadership ability and talent lead to a position of influence and power. With this feature, you should always maintain your integrity. It is important to remember that highly successful people also have fate lines that end on their Saturn mount, but in these cases perhaps the effort more than matches the reward.

Three Signs of Ambition

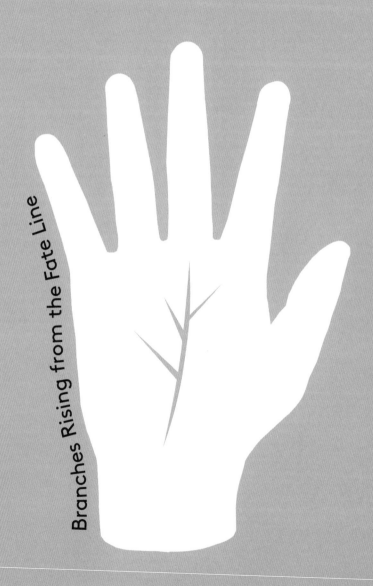

Branches Rising from the Fate Line

BRANCH RISING TO INDEX FINGER

You desire recognition and power, and have the self-belief to attain these. You are more driven than most, and you're motivated by competition, winning and earning the respect of your peers. Positions of leadership come your way – you are a political animal – and the cut and thrust of politics or management suit your competitive nature. You have the opportunity to make a positive difference to your environment, so make sure you are driven by strong principles and morality rather than by political expediency.

BRANCH RISING TO RING FINGER

This is an excellent indication that many of your dreams and ambitions will come true – but only when the necessary hard work has been done. Success will occur when preparation meets opportunity. Your creative instinct is strong. Being recognised for your talents is a prerequisite, and you will achieve some success in a creative field. Your head line will say much about how you achieve this acclaim, and your palm shape will indicate what motivates you. Even in a business or teaching environment, you add creative flair and more than a little drama to your work.

BRANCH RISING TO LITTLE FINGER

This sign indicates wealth as a result of hard work. It suggests that you have worked hard to develop business acumen. Money and financial security are priorities, as they give you the freedom to determine your future. If your head line is curved rather than straight, it suggests wealth can be yours if you take control of your finances, but you may have needed to learn business from scratch. You are a good deal-maker, and can charm others into submission with your skills of persuasion. A good income can be generated from writing, sales, promotions or acting as an agent.

THE MINOR HAND LINES & MARKINGS

Most hands have a variety of other markings – special line formations that can indicate talents, additional characteristics and drives. In this chapter, we'll be looking at the most important minor lines and formations.

THE APOLLO LINE

The Apollo line (a), which runs up to the ring finger, has much to say about your sense of personal fulfilment when found on the left hand, and your attitude to success and creativity when found on the right. It is an artistic marking, so those of you who have it strongly marked, or of considerable length in the hand, will enjoy creative or artistic pursuits.

Traditional palmists saw it as a sign of fame and fortune, but it is not always found on the hands of celebrities and the wealthy, but rather on those who enjoy their lives and their work. When the Apollo line is absent, this shows that you are quite hard to please. You are always on the lookout for something or someone who will bring happiness into your life, rather than working out a way to make yourself happy and content. The good news about the Apollo line is that it will appear or develop on the hand when you are striving to enjoy life and being more creative.

The Apollo line is often found amid many fine lines on water hands, and therefore should be afforded less significance. It is rare in its complete form on earth and fire hands, so keep this in mind, too. In most hands, it is only found above the heart line, and this suggests that your later years bring you a measure of happiness and personal contentment.

The best way to understand this line is to look at your palm shape, as this will show you what you strive for and what's most important to you. Having an Apollo line on an earth hand suggests material security could be attained. On an air hand, it might indicate the publication of a book or recognition of your ideas. On a fire hand, it could suggest attention and a position of power. On a water hand, it's most likely to reflect inner calm and a feeling of really making a difference to the world around you.

THE RING OF SOLOMON

Found on the fleshy mound under your index finger (b), this marking of psychological insight indicates that you have good people skills and an ability to understand others' motivations. It is likely that you will use this gift of psychological understanding in your work, perhaps being drawn into the fields of psychology or self-development. Or maybe you are an amateur psychologist to friends or the office advice-giver, always ready to lend an ear and give an opinion. You are naturally geared towards delving beyond what others say and do – a psychological detective always looking for hidden meanings and clues as to underlying emotions. Simply put, you want to know what makes others tick but can sometimes scramble around looking for motives that are not there. At best, you offer words of wisdom and inspiration that others can relate to. These words may come to you in intuitive flashes.

THE TEACHER'S SQUARE

This square or box-like marking (c, also found on the fleshy mound under the index finger) suggests an ability to teach and inspire others. You look for work in which you are able to communicate information with clarity and wisdom.

THE GIRDLE OF VENUS

This crescent-shaped marking (d) has suffered in reputation, with traditional palmists linking it to a lascivious, promiscuous nature. At its most profound, it can indicate the presence of a rare insight into human nature as well as an intuitive awareness of the future. If you have this line (particularly an unbroken one), you have a rare opportunity to develop psychic skills, whether it is having hunches about people or being able to predict events. Your psychic antennae are so sensitive that you can sense atmospheres and feel positive and negative vibrations. At worst, there may be a craving for excitement or stimulants that lands you in hot water.

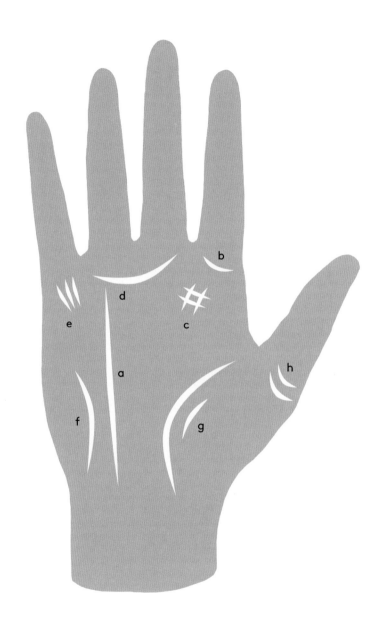

MEDICAL STIGMATA

With or without a bar connecting the trio of lines at the bottom, this marking (e, under the little finger) is often found on those who work in the caring professions.

THE BOW OF INTUITION

This is found on the percussion (outer) edge of the palm (f) and is often considered to be a sign of psychic ability. But it is more likely to be on the hands of those who make decisions based on hunches.

THE MARS LINE

Running a few centimetres inside the life line on the fleshy ball of the thumb (g), this reveals a combative person who never gives up. If you have one that runs a long way down alongside the life line, it shows that you recuperate fast and are able to bounce back from difficulties that would often defeat others. When the line is strong and long, you live for the battle, but remember that this does not make you the easiest person to live with. When the Mars line is stronger than the life line, you may have built up an arsenal of anger and resentment about life. Find avenues to release these potentially self-destructive traits.

THE FAMILY RING

Two rings at the base of the thumb (h) are said to show strong family ties and lifelong connections with family. More interesting are the lines that run from the lower ring towards the life line. When they stop at the life line or Mars line, they register the various family dramas that impact your life. If they travel beyond the life line and up towards one of the fingers, this indicates an event that changes your life – for example, if travelling towards the ring finger, they may show the birth of a child or the beginning of a profound relationship.

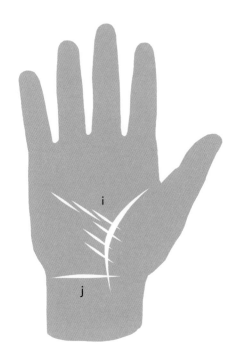

THE HEALTH LINE

This line (i) originates from under the little finger and heads diagonally towards the life line. Sometimes it is one clear diagonal line, suggesting you have a good sense of daily rhythms and energy levels and which foods agree with you. When it's a series of broken lines (see diagram), it is more likely to suggest a nervous disposition – someone who is an emotional seesaw.

THE ALLERGY LINE

This line (j) usually appears from the outside edge of the palm and heads towards the life line. It is a warning of sensitivity or addiction to chemicals (especially nicotine), alcohol and foods (particularly processed sugar foods). If you also have a girdle of Venus, be extra careful not to become dependent on drugs, pills or alcohol.

Travel & Relationship Lines

On the next few pages, you'll learn how to see the main signs for voyages as well as the key markings and lines indicating relationships.

HORIZONTAL LINES ON THE OUTER EDGE OF THE PALM

These interesting lines (k) reveal a restless spirit as well as important and life-changing travels that take place before the age of 40. Interestingly, these lines are relative to your experiences. For example, those who cross the Atlantic each week will not have these travels indicated in their hands, but the country person who travels to a big city for a week will have a line if the journey has made a lasting impression.

BRANCHES OFF THE LIFE LINE

These lines (l) show a strong desire to travel. They will pinpoint times when you make important travels and changes of residence. Interestingly, the more you have, the more you search for stability and permanence in your life. Often these lines will be found at least halfway down the life line, suggesting travels or moves abroad in later years. The strongest lines will show the most important trips away, and if the line is stronger than the life line, you may move location, or even to another country, at this time and not return.

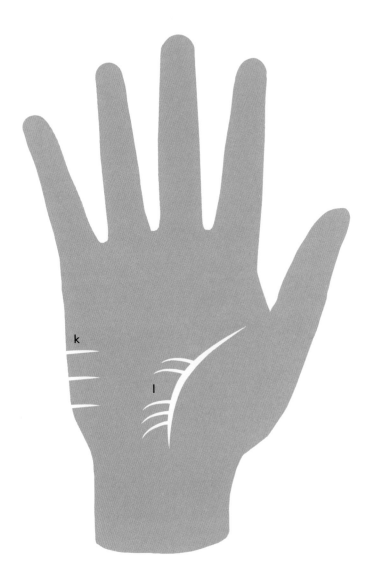

LINE FROM INSIDE THE LIFE LINE HEADING TOWARDS THE HEART LINE

This is a relationship line (m) that's an indication of a true meeting of minds. Someone comes into your life at a time, perhaps after a sheltered upbringing, when you are willing to make a major commitment. When a similar line follows further down the life line but is, in fact, broken, this may be a time when the relationship faces a make-or-break period, often because of an emotional upheaval following some kind of breakdown in communication.

SHORT LINE(S) JOINING THE FATE LINE

This influence line (n) can show anyone who joins your path (fate line) and influences your journey. When a line joins the fate line from the direction of the thumb, it shows a personal commitment (or influence from a family member) that shapes your personal (left hand) or professional (right hand) life. When it sweeps in from the outer edge of the hand, expect someone to enter from your sphere of work. With arranged marriages, there is a belief that love matches are shown as influence lines from the outer edge, while strictly arranged unions come from the direction of the family area (the thumb).

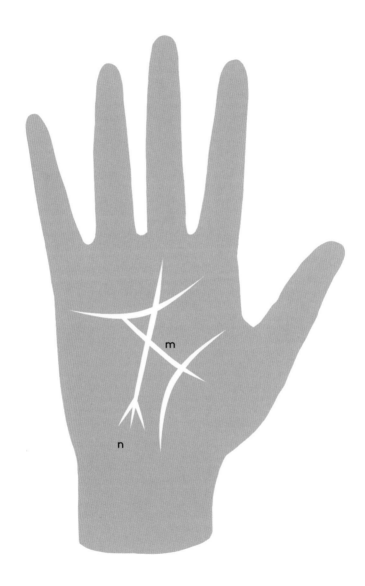

The Palm Reading Guide   109

Marriage Lines

These lines are, according to old palmistry books, supposed to represent marriages, although nowadays they symbolise all romantic relationships. But because these markings are under the little finger, they are linked to people who are on your mind – whether you have met them or not! (I've seen markings here from clients who have been unhealthily obsessed with a celebrity who, in their mind, is in some kind of relationship with them.) So they are not predictors of marriage but of where we place our attention.

The depth and length of the lines are relative to the depth of your feelings about the people – and the length of time they affect you – rather than the actual length of the relationship. Not all your romantic relationships will necessarily show up – only the ones that have really affected you. The markings on your left hand will be more significant when noting your deep love commitments.

To time these lines, divide the area into three sections of 25 years. The lowest section will deal with early relationships that moulded your sexuality and love desires and needs. The middle section is from the mid- to late 20s to mid-life, during which one or two significant lines show up even if you have had many relationships. Finally, the last third will trace those possible commitments you could have into your later years.

These lines show possible commitments, chances that are available (that is, possibilities 'in your mind') but, of course, you don't have to act on them or end existing relationships. Don't forget that relationship choices are certainly 'in your hands'. Sometimes lines appear twice because your partner has re-entered your life or you have taken up a new path with them. Either way, it feels like a new way of relating or a chance to explore other avenues together.